Start With A Story... by

Myself

Creating
Music, Movement & Drama
for Early Years

CHESTER MUSIC
PART OF THE MUSIC SALES GROUP

LONDON / NEW YORK / PARIS / SYDNEY / COPENHAGEN / BERLIN / MADRID / HONG KONG / TOKYO

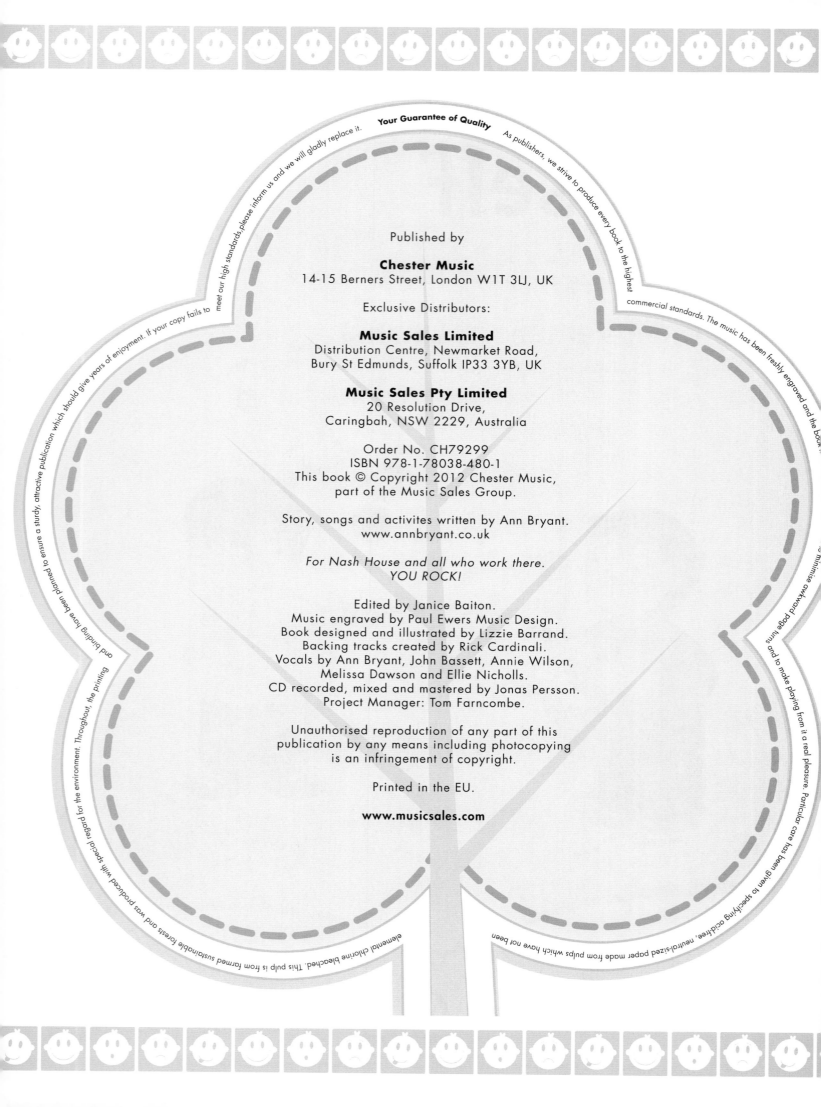

Published by

Chester Music
14-15 Berners Street, London W1T 3LJ, UK

Exclusive Distributors:

Music Sales Limited
Distribution Centre, Newmarket Road,
Bury St Edmunds, Suffolk IP33 3YB, UK

Music Sales Pty Limited
20 Resolution Drive,
Caringbah, NSW 2229, Australia

Order No. CH79299
ISBN 978-1-78038-480-1
This book © Copyright 2012 Chester Music,
part of the Music Sales Group.

Story, songs and activites written by Ann Bryant.
www.annbryant.co.uk

For Nash House and all who work there.
YOU ROCK!

Edited by Janice Baiton.
Music engraved by Paul Ewers Music Design.
Book designed and illustrated by Lizzie Barrand.
Backing tracks created by Rick Cardinali.
Vocals by Ann Bryant, John Bassett, Annie Wilson,
Melissa Dawson and Ellie Nicholls.
CD recorded, mixed and mastered by Jonas Persson.
Project Manager: Tom Farncombe.

Printed in the EU.

www.musicsales.com

Contents

About the author

Since graduating from the Royal College of Music and gaining a diploma in Dalcroze Eurhythmics, Ann Bryant has been teaching music, movement and drama. For over twenty years she has specialised in Early Years and Key Stage 1, writing many primary school music resources and leading workshops both in the UK and abroad. During this time Ann has also developed a highly successful career as a children's author, publishing over 110 books in these two distinct fields. Ann is a great believer in the integrated arts. She says, 'I love it when the two sides of my career overlay and overlap, which is why I have so enjoyed producing the four books in the *Start With A Story* series!'

'I used these books with my Nursery and love the way that alongside the fabulous music, drama and dance ideas, all aspects of the Early Years Foundation stage are covered.

The songs were hugely popular, catchy and easy to pick up and we have been introduced to a wide range of musical genres including traditional nursery rhymes, modern action rhymes, classical music, rap and jazz.

The stories in the books are written in a fun way that generates lots of discussion, and having the activities coming out of the story works brilliantly and gave us lots of ideas of our own, too!

But the best thing about the books is that you can use as much or as little as you like, since they are very easy to dip in and out of, so you can pick the bits that best suit you and your class at the time!'

Johanna Scanlon
Head of Nursery

Getting ready to sing – a handy tip
Pretend you are a balloon slowly fizzling as your air goes out. Make a long slow 's' sound as you let your air out and feel your whole upper body caving in. Now *very slowly* uncurl and straighten right up. Then you are ready to start singing.

Introduction

Each of the four books in the series has been specially written with a story as the starting point. The stories are utterly suitable for the Early Years age group, with familiar settings but also opportunities for learning. The books can be used in any order and can be dipped into or worked through. From the story emerge songs, poems and many other music and drama activities which all embrace and help promote the Early Years Foundation Stage curriculum requirements of:

- Personal, social and emotional development

- Communication, language and literacy

- Problem solving, reasoning and numeracy

- Knowledge and understanding of the world

- Physical development

- Creative development.

The story – **A Week In The Life Of Tommy Mac** – is presented twice in this book. First, we have the whole story. Then, we have each chapter again, alongside a song and a range of music, movement and/or drama activities.

The wonderful musical arrangements on the CD turn every song into a magical adventure. Look out for this logo 💿 which shows where there is music for the activities. Even without the book, you are sure to relish the CD!

The activities are set out in chapters like the story itself. Some might act as springboards for other work. Many bear repetition and often benefit from it. The generic ideas which don't particularly relate to music/movement/drama appear in boxes with Mrs Drabble to point them out. Feel free to develop the ideas as much or as little as you want. All you need is a space, a selection of percussion instruments and a CD player.

Early Years Settings leaders with no music training will find these books very easy to use. It may be that there are ideas in here which you never realised were musically valid! Specialists will welcome the fresh approach of integrating music with drama, movement and literacy, and highlighting an abundance of cross curricular opportunities.

A Week In The Life Of Tommy Mac

Chapter 1

On Wednesday morning Tommy woke up and remembered straight away that it was Nursery because he was a big boy now. So far he'd done two days at Nursery. It was OK, but it wasn't exactly the best thing in the whole wide world. Mummy told him to get dressed quickly so they wouldn't be late, and that put Tommy in a bit of a bad mood. He wasn't very good at doing things quickly.

At Nursery, Mrs Drabble was wearing her usual big smile. "Good morning, children," she said brightly.

"Good- mor-ning- Miss-is- Dra-bble," replied the children, very slowly and at exactly the same time like a load of talking tortoises.

"This morning we are going into the big hall to do some games," Mrs Drabble announced excitedly. "Let's make a lovely quiet line."

"Hooray!" everyone cried.

First it was 'Musical Mats,' then 'Pass the Big Ball' and 'Sailing down the River.' After that it was the obstacle race where you had to do things like climbing and balancing. When it was Tommy's turn to crawl through the big green caterpillar, he quickly knelt down and set off.

"This will be easy peasy," he said to himself.

But it wasn't easy. In fact it was really quite tricky and didn't feel like normal crawling at all.

"Hurry up, Tommy! Hurry up!" came lots of voices from outside the tunnel. Tommy tried to hurry up but he simply couldn't, and it took ages and ages before he came out of the other end of the caterpillar.

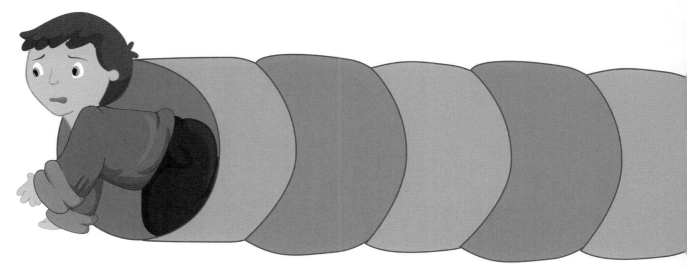

"You were *so* slow!" whispered a big boy called Jake. "Even a baby could go faster than you."

Tommy felt his cheeks getting hot. He couldn't forget those words the whole day long.

Chapter 2

On Thursday morning at Nursery, Mrs Drabble showed the children some pictures by a famous artist called L.S. Lowry. The children noticed how Lowry liked painting people who looked like tiny matchstick men, all very much the same. Next Mrs Drabble asked the children to make pictures of their own with lots of little matchstick people. First you had to choose a pale colour and cover the whole paper with that colour, then paint your little figures on the top in black. Tommy chose yellow for his colour but he went on and on and on painting until his paper was soggy, so when he started to paint the little men on the top, the paper tore. Tommy was cross with himself, but luckily no one was looking so he hurriedly crumpled the paper into a tight little ball. Then — uh-oh!

Mrs Drabble was coming over and there was no time to put the ball in the bin. There was only one thing to be done. Tommy sat on it.

"Where's your picture, Tommy?" asked Mrs Drabble.

"You... you didn't give me any paper," said Tommy, looking down.

"I thought I'd given everyone paper," Mrs Drabble said with a frown. "Never mind, pop and get a piece from my table."

Tommy tried to pick up the ball of crumpled paper as he stood up, but he was too late.

Mrs Drabble spotted it. "Oh dear," she said sadly as she uncrumpled the soggy paper. "You weren't telling the truth, were you Tommy?"

Tommy stared at the floor. For the rest of the day, he couldn't forget the sadness in Mrs Drabble's voice.

Chapter 3

On Friday morning when Tommy was having breakfast he told his mum he didn't want to go to Nursery.

"Why is that?" Mum asked.

Tommy couldn't explain. Mum might be cross about the lie he'd told. "Because I *don't!*" he answered grumpily.

"Have some more breakfast. You've only had three bites of toast."

Tommy was getting crosser. Toast wouldn't make anything better. "No!" he shouted.

"Don't be rude!" said his mum. "I hope you're not rude like that at Nursery."

It was a horrible day at Nursery. In the morning Mrs Drabble took the children on a walk to listen to the sounds outside. Tommy didn't enjoy it because Jake kept pulling faces at him. Neither did he enjoy the 'name' game that they played when they got back, nor the story about the very hungry caterpillar. And when it came to lunchtime, to make matters worse, he saw that his mum had forgotten to pack him his usual juice drink.

Jake was sitting next to him peering into Tommy's lunchbox. "Tommy hasn't got a drink!" he announced loudly, a big grin on his face.

Tommy felt a knot of crossness in his tummy.

"Would you like some water, Tommy?" asked Mrs Drabble.

"Water's boring," whispered Jake.

The knot of crossness inside Tommy's tummy grew bigger. "No!" he shouted at Mrs Drabble. "Water's boring!"

"Tommy! That was very rude!" said Mrs Drabble. "Now, let's try again. Would you like some water?"

Tommy scowled at her.

"You're not leaving this table until you've said no thank you," Mrs Drabble told Tommy.

Later when everyone was playing outside and Tommy was still sitting at the table he mumbled. "Can I have some water please?"

So Mrs Drabble got Tommy some water and said she was pleased he was a nice polite boy now. But Tommy was still cross. He thought the water was horrible and Jake was horrible and everything in the whole wide world was horrible.

Chapter 4

"Hurray, it's Saturday! No Nursery!" Tommy said to himself when he woke up the next morning.

After breakfast Tommy and his mum and dad went to the market. Tommy loved the market. It was busy and noisy and bright, and there was so much to see — toys and books and clothes and food. At the DVD stall Mum bought the film of *The Invisible Giant* and Tommy couldn't wait to get home to watch it.

That afternoon it rained. It was also very cold and Dad made a log fire in the sitting room. Then he made a lovely fish pie and a cheesecake for tea. Mum practised her flute, and then watched the football on her computer and Tommy snuggled into a beanbag and watched *The Invisible Giant*. It was brilliant.

At teatime he told Mum and Dad all about the film.

"The giant could turn himself invisible whenever he wanted. Then he crept 'round playing tricks on everyone!"

"I see," said Dad. "So he was a baddy."

Tommy frowned. "I'm not sure if he was a baddy, because he was quite lonely. He said he wanted a friend, only he didn't know how to get one. I think that's why he played tricks all the time. To make people like him."

"Oh dear," said Mum. "Did he get a friend in the end?"

Tommy nodded. "It was a boy called Kit. The giant played the worst tricks of all on Kit but Kit knew it was only because he was lonely and didn't know how to get a friend."

"So it was a happy ending," said Mum.

Tommy thought about the film in bed that night. For some reason or other the giant made him think of Jake. Was Jake lonely like the giant?

Chapter 5

Sunday was a bright sunny day but still a bit cold. Tommy woke up with a plan. He was going to practise crawling through tunnels until he could do it really quickly. So after breakfast he carried all the plastic garden chairs from the patio and put them side by side in a long line, then he crawled through the middle of all the legs. It was a bit awkward at first and he had to go quite slowly, but by his fourth go he was able to go a little quicker. Then on his fifth go he knocked two chairs over, which made him grumpy.

Luckily the cat from next door came along at that moment and wanted to be stroked, so Tommy's crossness soon melted away.

In the afternoon he went to Auntie Leila and Uncle Mark's house with Mum and Dad. It was all right playing with his cousin Lulu, except that she always insisted they play at least one game of 'house' and Tommy didn't like that.

"You be the dad," said Lulu, "and I'll be the mum. I'm cooking. What are you doing?"

"Cooking," said Tommy.

"No, dads don't cook," snapped Lulu. "Watch the football or something."

"Dads do cook," said Tommy firmly, starting to make a pretend cake.

Lulu watched him for a bit and then her bottom lip started trembling. Tommy felt sorry for her. He didn't want her to cry so he switched on the pretend TV and shouted, "Referee!"

A few minutes later when Tommy and Lulu were both colouring in Peppa Pig, Lulu suddenly pulled something out of her pocket and handed it to Tommy. "You can have this. I don't want it," she said.

Tommy's eyes nearly popped out of his head. It was a little model of the Invisible Giant. "Cool!" he said.
"Thank you, Lulu!"

Chapter 6

On Monday at Nursery Jake wanted to sit next to Tommy,
which made Tommy feel rather nervous.

"Your nose is running," Jake whispered.

Tommy quickly felt his nose. It was perfectly dry.

"Ha ha, I was tricking you!" said Jake.

Tommy thought about the invisible giant and all his tricks.

"There's a spider on your head!" said Jake.

Tommy didn't like spiders. He quickly brushed his hand over his head
and a black plastic spider fell on the floor. "Hee hee, that was a good trick,
wasn't it!" said Jake, grinning.

Mrs Drabble came over and said, "What's going on here?"

"Jake put a spider on my head," explained Tommy, pointing at it.
"I don't really like spiders."

"It was a joke!" said Jake, still grinning.

"Well, I don't find it funny and neither does Tommy," said Mrs Drabble.

Jake's bottom lip started to tremble. Tommy felt a bit sorry for him but then quickly changed his mind about that. Why should he feel sorry for someone who kept playing tricks on him and also told everyone in a big voice that he didn't have a drink in his lunch box?

Later when Tommy was at home, he decided to have another practice crawling through the garden chair legs because it was going to be games in the hall the next day. That's what Mrs Drabble had said, and Tommy didn't want Jake calling him slower than a baby again. He practised it six times and every time he got better and better.

When Tommy went to bed he looked at the model of the invisible giant that was sitting on his chest of drawers, and had a brilliant idea.

Chapter 7

On Tuesday at Nursery, it was good fun doing games in the big hall, and best of all was crawling through the tunnel.

"Wow! Well done, Tommy!" said Mrs Drabble. "You were fast as a ferret!"

When Jake had his go he was much slower and when he came out of the tunnel he was wearing a big scowl on his face. "I got stuck!" he said.

Later when it was writing, Tommy wrote his name very neatly but Jake just scribbled all over his paper then screwed it up and threw it at Tommy's head.

"Ha ha. I got a goal!" he shouted. Then he pulled a horrible face and said, "Go on, tell the teacher! I don't care!" But Tommy didn't tell the teacher. Instead he pulled the invisible giant model out of his pocket and gave it to Jake. "It's a present," said Tommy.

"Don't you want it?" asked Jake in a softer voice than usual.

Tommy thought about that. He *did* want it but he wanted Jake to have it more. "It's OK," he said. "You can have it."

When Mrs Drabble came over and saw Jake's paper she said, "Oh dear. Bad luck, Jake. Pop and get yourself another piece of paper."

Jake gave Tommy a big smile then went to find himself some more paper. When he came back he said to Tommy, "You're my best friend in the whole wide world."

Tommy felt very warm and fuzzy at that moment. "Do you want to come to tea at my house?" he asked Jake. "We could watch my DVD of *The Invisible Giant*."

Jake nodded hard.

Tommy grinned.

And Mrs Drabble smiled to herself and said, "Time for lunch everyone!"

Chapter 1

On Wednesday morning Tommy woke up and remembered straight away that it was Nursery because he was a big boy now. So far he'd done two days at Nursery. It was OK, but it wasn't exactly the best thing in the whole wide world. Mummy told him to get dressed quickly so they wouldn't be late, and that put Tommy in a bit of a bad mood. He wasn't very good at doing things quickly.

At Nursery, Mrs Drabble was wearing her usual big smile. "Good morning, children," she said brightly.

"Good- mor-ning- Miss-is- Dra-bble," replied the children, very slowly and at exactly the same time like a load of talking tortoises.

"This morning we are going into the big hall to do some games," Mrs Drabble announced excitedly. "Let's make a lovely quiet line."

"Hooray!" everyone cried.

First it was 'Musical Mats,' then 'Pass the Big Ball' and 'Sailing down the River.' After that it was the obstacle race where you had to do things like climbing and balancing. When it was Tommy's turn to crawl through the big green caterpillar, he quickly knelt down and set off.

"This will be easy peasy," he said to himself.

But it wasn't easy. In fact it was really quite tricky and didn't feel like normal crawling at all.

"Hurry up, Tommy! Hurry up!" came lots of voices from outside the tunnel. Tommy tried to hurry up but he simply couldn't, and it took ages and ages before he came out of the other end of the caterpillar.

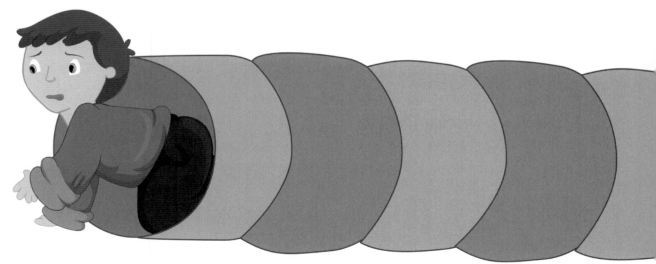

"You were *so* slow!" whispered a big boy called Jake. "Even a baby could go faster than you."

Tommy felt his cheeks getting hot. He couldn't forget those words the whole day long.

We're Sailing Down The River

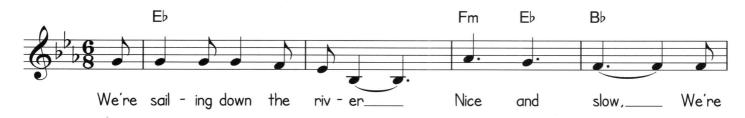

We're sail - ing down the riv - er_____ Nice and slow,_____ We're

sail - ing down the riv - er_____ Nice and slow._____ We're

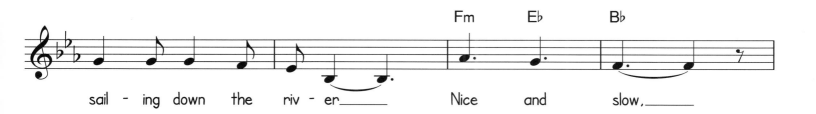

sail - ing down the riv - er_____ Nice and slow,_____

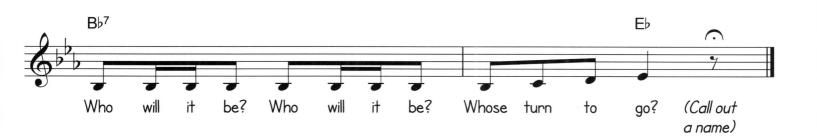

Who will it be? Who will it be? Whose turn to go? *(Call out a name)*

Let's Sing!
(CD tracks 1 and 2)

🐜 This song is reflecting the fact that Tommy went so slowly through the tunnel.

🐜 Use CD track 1 to learn how the song goes. The backing track allows for five children to 'swim' round, but you might prefer to sing unaccompanied in order to give more children a go.

🐜 All the children sit in a long line one behind the other as though in a long narrow boat. The first part of the song is very leisurely. The children can sway gently, either side to side or backwards and forwards as long as everyone is going the same way! After singing 'Whose turn to go?' the children listen to see whose name you call out, e.g. Ben. That child then gets up and 'swims' quickly down the line and back up the other side and sits back down in his place whilst the other children clap in time to the faster beat of the music on the CD.

Speedy and slow singing

🐜 Pick any song you all know and try singing it at different speeds.

🐜 Decide which speed you like best and why. Maybe the words sounded rushed or the music sounded messy if the speed was too fast. Maybe the words of a bright cheerful song sound odd if they are sung too slowly.

Musical mats

The children played this game in the story. Put a big mat down. Have a chair at each end of the room. The children are going to skip or gallop in a circle so that part of their route involves skipping over the mat, then round the chair and round the other chair.

Let the children choose a CD with the right style of music for skipping/galloping. The beat needs to fit.

Pause the music whenever you want. Whoever is on the mat at the time is out.

Musical statues and musical bumps

These two games are also musically valid because the children must listen for when the music stops and react quickly. Make the game more challenging by giving the children definite actions to do whilst the music is playing. You might chose two actions which the children must alternate, doing four of each, e.g. four punches up in the air with alternate hands, followed by four slaps of the floor with alternate hands. Again, you need to choose music which will suit the actions.

Winning and losing

This is a good opportunity to talk about how you feel when you're eliminated. It's important not to boast if you're successful and not to worry if you're not. It's only a game!

Chapter 1 Activities

Slow as a tortoise

Tommy was slow at going through the tunnel. Talk about animals which move slowly.

Can you crawl as slowly as a tortoise?

What is the *opposite* of slow? Talk about animals which move quickly.

Can you run as fast as a cheetah?

Carnival Of The Animals
(CD tracks 3 and 4)

Listen to 'The Tortoise' and 'The Mules' from *Carnival of the Animals* by Saint Saëns. These two pieces of music show the slow and fast contrast very effectively.

The tune in 'The Tortoise' is played on the cello. The piano is the accompanying instrument. Can you find other pictures of cellos apart from the one on this page? Any other cello music? A very famous piece of cello music is also part of *Carnival of the Animals* – 'The Swan'. What instrument can you hear in 'The Mules'?

For a joke, Saint Saëns imitated the tune of the famous 'Can-can' music from *Orpheus in the Underworld* by Offenbach for 'The Tortoise', but in 'The Tortoise' it is played very slowly as a contrast!

Rolling balls slowly

Have the children sit in a row side by side in front of you but a little distance away from you. Take a large soft ball and roll it slowly towards the first child. That child must to roll it back, trying to achieve the same speed. Repeat with the other children.

Ask the children to get in pairs. The partners roll the balls between each other trying to roll slowly and accurately.

Watch one pair at a time. The children must aim to roll the ball at the same speed as their partner – a very slow speed. This takes a great deal of control.

Choose the pair who achieve this best, and as they roll to each other, make a long slow sound, e.g. 'Oooooh' then for the return roll 'aaaaaaah.'

What other sounds can you think of? It might be easiest to simply put a different consonant on the front of 'oooooh' 'aaaah', e.g. 'boooo' 'baaaa' 'woooo' 'waaaa' etc.

Have two pairs rolling the ball at the same time, still keeping very slow and controlled. Divide the rest of the children into two groups. One group makes two long slow sounds to accompany one pair, and the other group similarly accompanies the other pair but starting with the 'aaaah' sound. This makes a nice sound collage.

slowly →

Chapter 2

On Thursday morning at Nursery, Mrs Drabble showed the children some pictures by a famous artist called L.S. Lowry. The children noticed how Lowry liked painting people who looked like tiny matchstick men, all very much the same. Next Mrs Drabble asked the children to make pictures of their own with lots of little matchstick people. First you had to choose a pale colour and cover the whole paper with that colour, then paint your little figures on the top in black. Tommy chose yellow for his colour but he went on and on and on painting until his paper was soggy, so when he started to paint the little men on the top, the paper tore. Tommy was cross with himself, but luckily no one was looking so he hurriedly crumpled the paper into a tight little ball. Then — uh-oh!

Mrs Drabble was coming over and there was no time to put the ball in the bin. There was only one thing to be done. Tommy sat on it.

"Where's your picture, Tommy?" asked Mrs Drabble.

"You… you didn't give me any paper," said Tommy, looking down.

"I thought I'd given everyone paper," Mrs Drabble said with a frown. "Never mind, pop and get a piece from my table."

Tommy tried to pick up the ball of crumpled paper as he stood up, but he was too late.

Mrs Drabble spotted it. "Oh dear," she said sadly as she uncrumpled the soggy paper. "You weren't telling the truth, were you Tommy?"

Tommy stared at the floor. For the rest of the day, he couldn't forget the sadness in Mrs Drabble's voice.

There's A Dragon In The Sky

CD tracks 5 and 6

1. There's a dra-gon in the sky And I am down be-low, There's a

dra-gon in the sky And he's call-ing out hel-lo! Is it true what I said? Is it

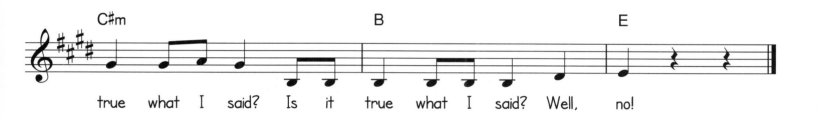

true what I said? Is it true what I said? Well, no!

2. There's a polar bear at school
   As happy as can be,
   There's a polar bear at school
   And he's dancing round with me.

   Is it true what I said?
   Is it true what I said?
   Is it true what I said?

   Well, no!

3. There's a daisy in the grass
   It's yellow and it's white,
   There's a daisy in the grass
   And it's such a pretty sight.

   Is it true what I said?
   Is it true what I said?
   Is it true what I said?

   Well, yes!

Let's play!

🐛 Take turns to play to the beat of the three verses of the song with the CD. All play together on 'Is it true what I said' then when it comes to the answer, play quietly for 'Well no!' and loudly for 'Well yes!'

Let's Sing!
(CD tracks 5 and 6)

🐛 This song is reflective of the lie that Tommy told Mrs Drabble. Add more verses based on things and people you can see around you.

🐛 Talk about why Tommy told the lie. What would have been a better thing to do?

Find the odd one out

🐛 In the Lowry paintings all the people *look* very similar. This activity involves making shakers which all *sound* very similar, apart from one.

🐛 If possible all the shakers should be made using identical small containers with the same amount of the same filling e.g. dried rice, dried pulses. Make the odd one out by putting a heavier filling, e.g. tiny pebbles, into the *same kind of container*, so there is no visible clue as to which is the odd one out. Make sure the containers are definitely secure so that even the most vigorous shaking won't allow the filling to escape!

🐛 Talk about the sound of the shakers using words such as light, feathery, wispy, swishing, quiet, whispery: and the sound of the odd one out, using words such as crunchy, heavy, loud, hard.

🐛 The children, apart from one, should sit in a circle, each with a shaker in front of them. At a signal from you, all the children play their respective shakers. The child with the heavier one must try not to give away that (s)he has the odd one out! The child without a shaker should walk around the inside of the circle listening out for the louder sound. How quickly can they find it?

The paintings of L.S. Lowry

Look at some paintings of L.S. Lowry. Notice all the 'matchstick people'. See how they are placed in the picture.

Create the largest possible rectangular space on the classroom floor and imagine this is the background of one particular Lowry painting, and the children are the matchstick people. Decide which side of the rectangle is the 'top'. Can the children arrange themselves as though they are in the picture?

Now think of other ways of arranging the matchstick people and group the children accordingly. They might be in pairs, in clusters, in the corners, in the middle. What ideas do the children have for the artistic arrangement?

Let's paint!

Try exactly the same art activity as the one Mrs Drabble set for her class! Now the children have had practice of arranging themselves as matchstick people, they should think about what pattern of matchstick people they would like to paint on their own pictures.

They might like to try out various ideas to see how the patterns look using little counters or broken bits of matches.

Celebrate difference!

Talk about how much more interesting it is that we all look very different in reality. There is scope for lots of discussion here.

Sometimes if we wear the same clothes it makes us look more like a group than a set of individuals, e.g. school uniform, people in a swimming pool, dancers in the same outfits on stage. Can the children think of any more examples of this?

Chapter 2 Activities

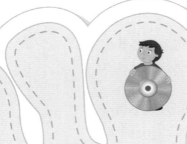

Let's move!
(CD track 7)

🐛 Play CD track 7. This is a very quiet piece of music. Listen to the music while you look at a few of the Lowry paintings. Does the music make you think of lots of little people all going about their business? Talk about where everyone might be going.

🐛 Now practise jogging round (without shoes, to keep the volume down, and possibly without socks to prevent slipping). Travel over a very tiny distance doing neat little steps, picking your knees up in time with the music. When everyone does it together, do the children make too much noise for you to hear the music?

🐛 Try with just one child. Can you hear the music? Keep adding more and more children and see how many can do the jogging at the same time without preventing you from hearing the music. This is very good for careful listening, mood matching and self-discipline.

Different beat, same beat

🐛 This activity is reflective of the 'sameness' of the little matchstick men in the Lowry paintings. All travel round the room doing a mixture of skipping jogging, striding, and when *you* start playing your drum, everyone must walk to your steady beat.

🐛 Try that with musical instruments. Everyone can play at any speed they want so it makes a messy sound but when you do a certain visual signal, all the children must play to the same beat as you.

Spot The Difference

Can you spot the six differences between these two pictures?

21

Chapter 3

On Friday morning when Tommy was having breakfast he told his mum he didn't want to go to Nursery.

"Why is that?" Mum asked.

Tommy couldn't explain. Mum might be cross about the lie he'd told. "Because I *don't!*" he answered grumpily.

"Have some more breakfast. You've only had three bites of toast."

Tommy was getting crosser. Toast wouldn't make anything better. "No!" he shouted.

"Don't be rude!" said his mum. "I hope you're not rude like that at Nursery."

It was a horrible day at Nursery. In the morning Mrs Drabble took the children on a walk to listen to the sounds outside. Tommy didn't enjoy it because Jake kept pulling faces at him. Neither did he enjoy the 'name' game that they played when they got back, nor the story about the very hungry caterpillar. And when it came to lunchtime, to make matters worse, he saw that his mum had forgotten to pack him his usual juice drink.

Jake was sitting next to him peering into Tommy's lunchbox. "Tommy hasn't got a drink!" he announced loudly, a big grin on his face.

Tommy felt a knot of crossness in his tummy.

"Would you like some water, Tommy?" asked Mrs Drabble.

"Water's boring," whispered Jake.

The knot of crossness inside Tommy's tummy grew bigger. "No!" he shouted at Mrs Drabble. "Water's boring!"

"Tommy! That was very rude!" said Mrs Drabble. "Now, let's try again. Would you like some water?"

Tommy scowled at her.

"You're not leaving this table until you've said no thank you," Mrs Drabble told Tommy.

Later when everyone was playing outside and Tommy was still sitting at the table he mumbled. "Can I have some water please?"

So Mrs Drabble got Tommy some water and said she was pleased he was a nice polite boy now. But Tommy was still cross. He thought the water was horrible and Jake was horrible and everything in the whole wide world was horrible.

Sounds Outside

CD tracks 8 and 9

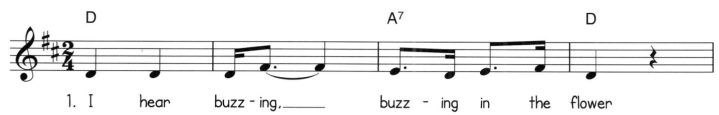

1. I hear buzz - ing,_____ buzz - ing in the flower

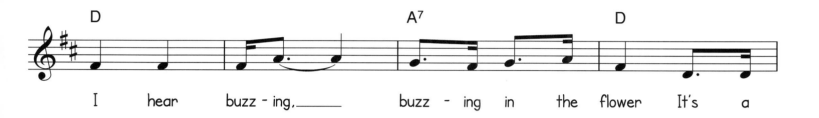

I hear buzz - ing,_____ buzz - ing in the flower It's a

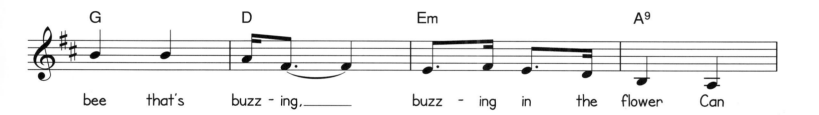

bee that's buzz - ing,_____ buzz - ing in the flower Can

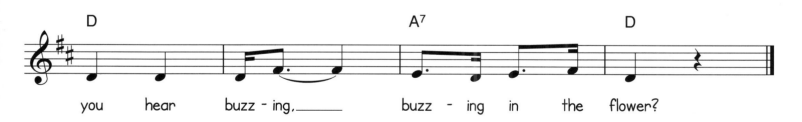

you hear buzz - ing,_____ buzz - ing in the flower?

2. I hear croaking, croaking in the pond
   I hear croaking, croaking in the pond
   It's a frog that's croaking, croaking in the pond
   Can you hear croaking, croaking in the pond?

3. I hear squeaking, squeaking in the leaves ...
   It's a mouse...

4. I hear tweeting, tweeting in the sky...
   It's a bird...

Let's Sing!
(CD tracks 8 and 9)

🐛 This song is based on the walk that Mrs Drabble and the children went on. First learn the song and sing it through all together. If you listen very carefully you might hear some buzzing, croaking, squeaking and tweeting!

🐛 Now organise the children into four groups. Tell each group what they are – bees, frogs, mice or birds. Everybody should sing every verse except their own, during which they should make the appropriate sound for their creature.

🐛 What other sounds might the children in the story have heard? How can you fit those into the tune of the song?

🐛 Can the children find a different suitable percussion sound (maybe homemade?) to accompany each verse?

Let's walk!

🐛 Have your own 'sound' walk. First talk about what sounds you might hear. Car engine? A plane? A train? People talking? Laughter? Shouting? A dog barking? Listen out for this list plus any others not on the list.

The Very Hungry Caterpillar

🐛 Mrs Drabble read the children the story of The Very Hungry Caterpillar. Try this action rhyme, fitting in actions as you want. Notice that the last verse has a different rhythm. Try to keep a strong beat throughout.

Caterpillar wriggle
Wriggle wriggle wriggle
Caterpillar wriggle
Now you've gone thinner!

Caterpillar munch
Munch munch munch
Caterpillar munch
Have a good dinner!

Caterpillar spin
Spin spin spin
Caterpillar spin
What a good spinner!

Wriggle and munch
and spin all day
And very very soon
You'll be wrapped
in a cocoon,
Then you'll turn into
a butterfly and
fly away!

Caterpillars and butterflies

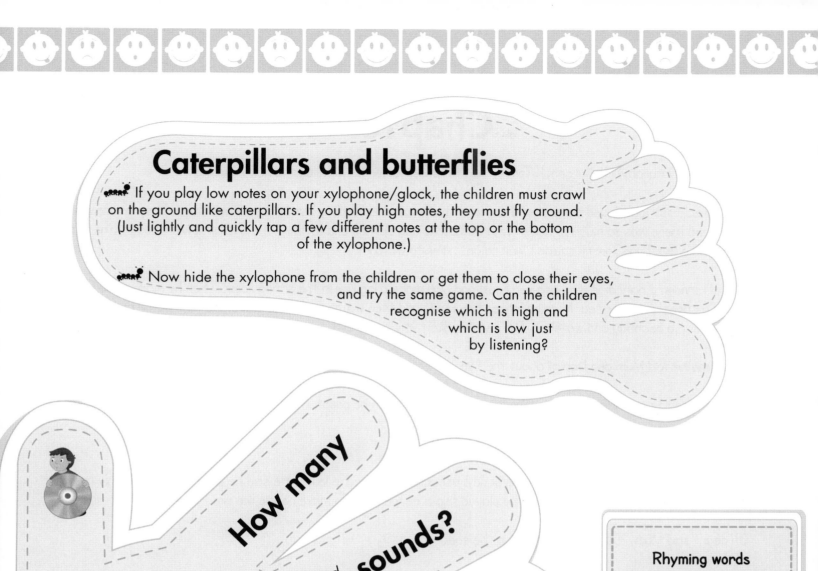

If you play low notes on your xylophone/glock, the children must crawl on the ground like caterpillars. If you play high notes, they must fly around. (Just lightly and quickly tap a few different notes at the top or the bottom of the xylophone.)

Now hide the xylophone from the children or get them to close their eyes, and try the same game. Can the children recognise which is high and which is low just by listening?

How many sounds?

Go through all the children's first names and emulate the rhythm of the name on the drum. Let them play their own names, tapping the right number of syllables as they say their names. Some will sound the same as each other. Listen to the examples on CD track 10. Some might have a skipping rhythm in their name.

Can the children recognise their names from the rhythms you tap on the drum? A child who thinks you have tapped his or her name should jump up immediately. The more you do this activity, the more children will come to recognise their own name and respond quickly to its rhythmic sound.

Rhyming words

In the story we heard about the 'Name Game'. The words 'name' and 'game' rhyme. Can you think of other pairs of rhyming words?

Try putting the words into little sentences, e.g.
I am a hen
Counting to ten

I am a horse
Galloping of course

I am a cow
Doing a bow

Chapter 4

"Hurray, it's Saturday! No Nursery!" Tommy said to himself when he woke up the next morning.

After breakfast Tommy and his mum and dad went to the market. Tommy loved the market. It was busy and noisy and bright, and there was so much to see — toys and books and clothes and food. At the DVD stall Mum bought the film of *The Invisible Giant* and Tommy couldn't wait to get home to watch it.

That afternoon it rained. It was also very cold and Dad made a log fire in the sitting room. Then he made a lovely fish pie and a cheesecake for tea. Mum practised her flute, and then watched the football on her computer and Tommy snuggled into a beanbag and watched *The Invisible Giant*. It was brilliant.

At teatime he told Mum and Dad all about the film.

"The giant could turn himself invisible whenever he wanted. Then he crept 'round playing tricks on everyone!"

"I see," said Dad. "So he was a baddy."

Tommy frowned. "I'm not sure if he was a baddy, because he was quite lonely. He said he wanted a friend, only he didn't know how to get one. I think that's why he played tricks all the time. To make people like him."

"Oh dear," said Mum. "Did he get a friend in the end?"

Tommy nodded. "It was a boy called Kit. The giant played the worst tricks of all on Kit but Kit knew it was only because he was lonely and didn't know how to get a friend."

"So it was a happy ending," said Mum.

Tommy thought about the film in bed that night. For some reason or other the giant made him think of Jake. Was Jake lonely like the giant?

The Extra Special Giant

CD tracks 11 and 12

1. You need an ex-tra spe-cial hat for a gi-ant.__ Ex-tra spe-cial hat for

me. Ex-tra spe-cial hat for a gi-ant.__ In my hat! Look at me!

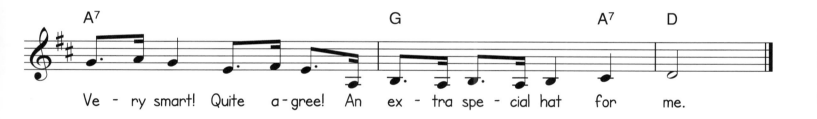

Ve - ry smart! Quite a-gree! An ex - tra spe - cial hat for me.

2. You need an extra special coat for a giant...

3. You need some extra special shoes for a giant...

4. You need an extra special chair for a giant...

5. You need an extra special bed for a giant...

Let's Sing!
(CD tracks 11 and 12)

As you sing, mime putting on the hat, the coat and the shoes, and admiring them, then sitting on the chair and lying on the bed and getting comfortable!

I went to the market...

In the story Tommy and his family went to the market. Play the game where the first person says, e.g., 'I went to the market and bought a loaf of bread,' and the second person says, 'I went to the market and bought a loaf of bread and a DVD.' Each child must try to remember the previous acquisitions and add another of his/her own.

Blowing and bowing

Do the children remember which instrument Tommy's mum practised? Talk about the flute. It is a blowing instrument.

What other blowing instruments have the children heard of? (recorder, piccolo, oboe, clarinet, bassoon, trumpet, trombone, horn, tuba)

Which stringed instruments have they heard of? (violin, viola, cello, double bass, guitar, banjo, ukulele, harp)

How are stringed instruments played? (with a bow or simply plucked)

Show pictures of any of these instruments, or better still see and hear live examples.

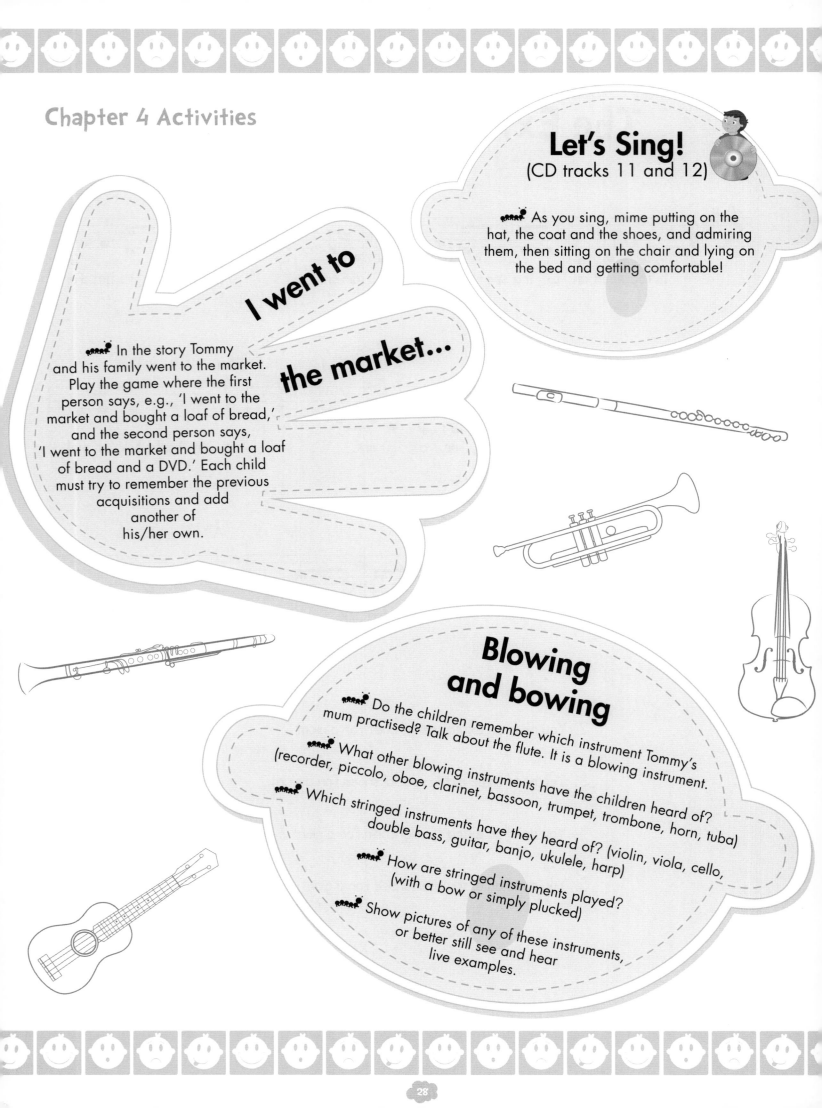

Stories with giants

What other stories do you know with giants in them? A favourite of mine is *Jim and the Beanstalk* by Raymond Briggs. In this story Jim equips the giant with a gigantic wig, some gigantic glasses and a set of gigantic false teeth!

Imagine you are a giant's wigmaker. Try this little action rhyme, using your hands imaginatively and nimbly:

**Thread this hair through bit by bit
Bit by bit, bit by bit.
Stretch it out to make it fit,
make it fit, make it fit.
Twizzle it up and twizzle it down
Scrunch it up and shake it around.**

What size are our steps?

🐛 Stride along like a giant taking big strides and notice how you are going more slowly.

🐛 Now take medium strides – being yourselves.

🐛 Now pretend you are a pixie and take tiny steps.

Three different steps

🐛 Divide the children into three groups. Allocate a corner of the room for the giant's home, one for the ordinary children, one for the pixies. You play the drum. Allocate a beat to each group – slow (giants), medium (children), quick (pixies). Then according to which beat you play, the giant, the children or the pixies should take steps around the room to match your beat. After giving each group a turn, change your beat unpredictably.

🐛 Have a sound signal which tells the children to swap corners and roles.

🐛 Now give the children instruments. Each group should have the same type of instrument. This time the relevant group joins in when they hear you playing their beat. You might have to put a hand up in the air to show when you are changing each time.

🐛 Again, have a set signal for swapping round. Everyone must creep like tiny mice to swap places.

The invisible giant's footsteps

Tell the children you are playing a drum to represent the giant's shoes. The children stride round the room in time to your beat. Keep it steady and slow. When you stop playing, the children must keep striding at the same slow speed just as an invisible giant would keep striding, but one wouldn't hear his footsteps. The children will inevitably speed up. The challenge is to try not to. After a few steps, pick up the beat on the drum, trying to resume with exactly the same slow beat as before. Did the children notice that they had sped up?

The invisible giant is singing!

Sing a song of your choice. When you put your hands up to say 'stop', the children must pretend that the giant is carrying on singing the song but we can't hear him because he is invisible, i.e. the children must continue to sing the song inside their heads without speeding up. This is called internalisation and is a fundamental music skill. It's never too soon to start developing the skill! When you raise your palms up, this is the signal to start singing out loud again as though the giant has returned. The aim is for all the children to be in the same place in the song when they resume singing!

Chapter 5

Sunday was a bright sunny day but still a bit cold. Tommy woke up with a plan. He was going to practise crawling through tunnels until he could do it really quickly. So after breakfast he carried all the plastic garden chairs from the patio and put them side by side in a long line, then he crawled through the middle of all the legs. It was a bit awkward at first and he had to go quite slowly, but by his fourth go he was able to go a little quicker. Then on his fifth go he knocked two chairs over, which made him grumpy.

Luckily the cat from next door came along at that moment and wanted to be stroked, so Tommy's crossness soon melted away.

In the afternoon he went to Auntie Leila and Uncle Mark's house with Mum and Dad. It was all right playing with his cousin Lulu, except that she always insisted they play at least one game of 'house' and Tommy didn't like that.

"You be the dad," said Lulu, "and I'll be the mum. I'm cooking. What are you doing?"

"Cooking," said Tommy.

"No, dads don't cook," snapped Lulu. "Watch the football or something."

"Dads do cook," said Tommy firmly, starting to make a pretend cake.

Lulu watched him for a bit and then her bottom lip started trembling. Tommy felt sorry for her. He didn't want her to cry so he switched on the pretend TV and shouted, "Referee!"

A few minutes later when Tommy and Lulu were both colouring in Peppa Pig, Lulu suddenly pulled something out of her pocket and handed it to Tommy. "You can have this. I don't want it," she said.

Tommy's eyes nearly popped out of his head. It was a little model of the Invisible Giant. "Cool!" he said.
"Thank you, Lulu!"

Football Is
The Game For Us!

CD tracks 13 and 14

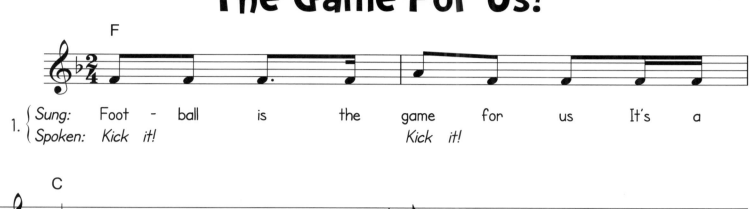

1. Sung: Foot - ball is the game for us It's a
   Spoken: Kick it! Kick it!

great game, it's a great game.
Kick it! Pen - al - ty!

Foot - ball is the game for us It's a
Kick it! Kick it!

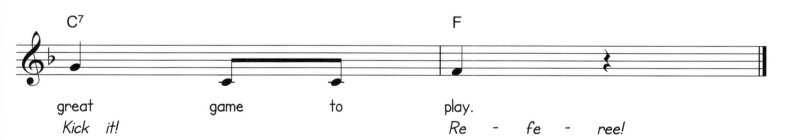

great game to play.
Kick it! Re - fe - ree!

Let's Sing!
(CD tracks 13 and 14)

🐜 This song is based on the mention of football in this chapter.

🐜 Join in with track 13 to learn how to sing the first part of the song and then how to chant the second part with plenty of vigour!

🐜 When you are confident, listen to how the two parts fit together and try to join in with half the class singing the first part at the same time as the other half chant the second part.

🐜 Finally try it with the backing track (14). This is a big challenge when there are no vocals to sing along with!

Action time!

🐜 Can you clap along with the slow claps on the CD?

🐜 Try doing, for example, two stamps or two 'air punches' before the clap each time, or invent a different action.

Jobs

In the story, why did Tommy choose cooking when he and Lulu were playing 'house'? Why didn't Lulu want Tommy to do cooking? Talk about the various jobs that mums and dads might do.

What jobs do the adults in the lives of the children in your class do? Pick up on any interesting ones. Talk about how being a mummy and being a daddy are jobs in themselves.

Football training

🐜 When footballers are training they jog and jump in all sorts of different ways – sideways, forwards and backwards, on the spot. There are four lots of eight beats in this song (i.e. the singing part and the chanting part combined). Use the backing track on the CD (14) and work out four different sets of moves relating to football training which will fit rhythmically into the music. Start with the actual moves you want, and then make them more abstract in feel so that when they are put together the whole thing becomes more of a dance.

Games
(CD track 15)

What are the children's favourite games? Make a bar chart to show the results of the survey.

In the 'old days', children used to play very different games. Listen to the piece on CD track 15, 'Trumpet and Drum' from the suite Children's Games by Bizet. There are twelve short pieces in the suite, all piano duets. The five most popular ones were scored for orchestra and put together to form the Petite Suite. They are named 'Trumpet and Drum', 'The Doll', 'The Top', 'Little Husband, Little Wife' and 'The Ball'.

Try joining in with a percussion accompaniment, tapping quietly to the strong beat.

Hobbies

Talk about what you like doing at weekends and in your spare time and what members of your family like to do.

If music is mentioned, get the children to be specific as to whether their family members like listening to music or actually playing instruments. Similarly with sport – watching it on TV or participating?

The baking song – We're going to make a cake!
(CD track 16)

In the story, Lulu is pretending to cook. Try singing the following lyrics to the traditional tune of 'The Farmer's In His Dell'. On track 16 we have given you just two verses to get the idea of the tune.

You might be able to think of new words. Notice how to fit monosyllabic words such as 'eggs', 'flour', 'marg' into the tune by singing, e.g., 'Put the eggs into the bowl'. For duosyllabic words such as 'raisins', 'cocoa' sing 'Put the raisins in the bowl'. By using 'in' with duosyllabic words and 'into' with monosyllabic words, you get the best rhythmic feel to the music.

We're going to make a cake
We're going to make a cake
Put the flour into the bowl
We're going to make a cake.

We're going to make a cake
We're going to make a cake
Put the raisins in the bowl
We're going to make a cake.

Chapter 6

On Monday at Nursery Jake wanted to sit next to Tommy,
which made Tommy feel rather nervous.

"Your nose is running," Jake whispered.

Tommy quickly felt his nose. It was perfectly dry.

"Ha ha, I was tricking you!" said Jake.

Tommy thought about the invisible giant and all his tricks.

"There's a spider on your head!" said Jake.

Tommy didn't like spiders. He quickly brushed his hand over his head
and a black plastic spider fell on the floor. "Hee hee, that was a good trick,
wasn't it!" said Jake, grinning.

Mrs Drabble came over and said, "What's going on here?"

"Jake put a spider on my head," explained Tommy, pointing at it.
"I don't really like spiders."

"It was a joke!" said Jake, still grinning.

"Well, I don't find it funny and neither does Tommy," said Mrs Drabble.

Jake's bottom lip started to tremble. Tommy felt a bit sorry for him but then quickly changed his mind about that. Why should he feel sorry for someone who kept playing tricks on him and also told everyone in a big voice that he didn't have a drink in his lunch box?

Later when Tommy was at home, he decided to have another practice crawling through the garden chair legs because it was going to be games in the hall the next day. That's what Mrs Drabble had said, and Tommy didn't want Jake calling him slower than a baby again. He practised it six times and every time he got better and better.

When Tommy went to bed he looked at the model of the invisible giant that was sitting on his chest of drawers, and had a brilliant idea.

It's Just A Trick!

CD tracks 17 and 18

1.The clouds are pur - ple hee hee hee, The

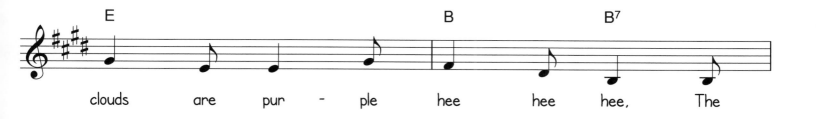

clouds are pur - ple hee hee hee, The

clouds are pur - ple hee hee hee, It's

just a trick, it's not true! *Phew!*

2. Your nose is running, hee hee hee...

3. My dad's a Martian, hee hee hee...

4. It's slugs for breakfast, hee hee hee...

Let's Sing!
(CD tracks 17 and 18)

This song will make the children laugh. Can they think of any more verses? I'm sure they'll have lots of ideas. It's fitting them into the music that's the tricky bit!

Incy wincy spider

In the story, Jake put a spider on Tommy's head. Here are two popular action rhymes, each about a spider.

**Incy Wincy Spider climbed up the water spout
Down came the rain and washed the spider out
Out came the sun and dried up all the rain
So Incy Wincy Spider climbed up the spout again!**

**I have a little spider and I'm very fond of him
He climbs on to my shoulder and then up to my chin
He crawls right down my arm, and then right down my leg.
And when he's tired I put my little spider in his bed.**
(Cup the spider in your other hand.)

(The second rhyme has been subtly changed from the original to give a more rhythmic feel to the words.)

Let's make spiders' webs!

Fill an empty shower gel bottle with PVA glue. Guide the child's hand in large circles on black card. Draw lines from the middle of the circle outwards with the glue. Cover with glitter. Shake off the excess. Back with silver paper and for a stunning effect, on black again.

Let's make spiders

Using Model Magic®, the children should roll balls. Paint them black or grey and use pipe cleaners or straws for legs, and polystyrene balls for eyes. Hang the finished spiders on fishing wire.

Daddy, mummy and baby spider

Stand up and using a deep voice, say 'I am daddy spider and I speak in a deep voice!' Sit down and using your normal voice, say, 'I am Mummy spider and I speak in a medium voice.' Stay sitting and speak in a whisper (but audibly) to say, 'I am baby spider and I speak in a whispery voice.'

Ask individual children their name, like this: 'Baby Spider Amir, what is your name?' Amir must then think quickly and answer you with the right voice quality, in this case a whisper: 'My name is Amir.' You can ask any question of any child, e.g. 'Mummy Spider Ellie, where do you live?' 'Daddy Spider Joe, what day is it today?'

This is very tricky for children to do and they often feel self-conscious at first, but really enjoy the thrill of getting it right!

Chapter 7

On Tuesday at Nursery, it was good fun doing games in the big hall, and best of all was crawling through the tunnel.

"Wow! Well done, Tommy!" said Mrs Drabble. "You were fast as a ferret!"

When Jake had his go he was much slower and when he came out of the tunnel he was wearing a big scowl on his face. "I got stuck!" he said.

Later when it was writing, Tommy wrote his name very neatly but Jake just scribbled all over his paper then screwed it up and threw it at Tommy's head.

"Ha ha. I got a goal!" he shouted. Then he pulled a horrible face and said, "Go on, tell the teacher! I don't care!" But Tommy didn't tell the teacher. Instead he pulled the invisible giant model out of his pocket and gave it to Jake. "It's a present," said Tommy.

"Don't you want it?" asked Jake in a softer voice than usual.

Tommy thought about that. He *did* want it but he wanted Jake to have it more. "It's OK," he said. "You can have it."

When Mrs Drabble came over and saw Jake's paper she said, "Oh dear. Bad luck, Jake. Pop and get yourself another piece of paper."

Jake gave Tommy a big smile then went to find himself some more paper. When he came back he said to Tommy, "You're my best friend in the whole wide world."

Tommy felt very warm and fuzzy at that moment. "Do you want to come to tea at my house?" he asked Jake. "We could watch my DVD of *The Invisible Giant.*"

Jake nodded hard.

Tommy grinned.

And Mrs Drabble smiled to herself and said, "Time for lunch everyone!"

Grumpy Stomps
And Happy Jumps

CD tracks 19 and 20

F   C   F   C

1. I'm   in   the   slump – y   grump – y   dumps   And   I

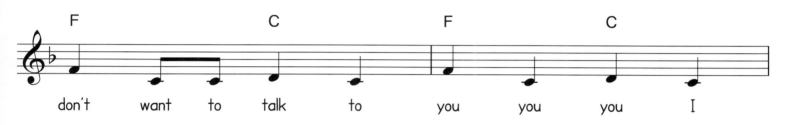

F   C   F   C

don't   want   to   talk   to   you   you   you   I

F   C   F

don't   want   to   talk   to   you.

I'm in the slumpy grumpy dumps
So this is what I do do do
So this is what I do.

I…

Stomp stomp stomp stomp
Stomp stomp stomp stomp
Stomp stomp stop!

2. I am a happy clappy chap
   And I just want to sing to you you you
   I just want to sing to you.

   I am a happy clappy chap
   So this is what I do do do
   So this is what I do.

   I…

   Jump jump jump jump
   Jump jump jump jump
   Jump jump stop!

Chapter 7 Activities

Let's Sing!
(CD tracks 19 and 20)

This is a great song for exploring the contrast between happy and grumpy. Stand still to sing the first two thirds of each verse, and then try to stomp/jump precisely in time to the beat. Don't forget to wear the appropriate expression on your face!

Try with half the class being the grumpy ones and the other half being the happy ones, and then swap.

Sad and happy music

Make up a piece of music on percussion instruments of your choice. Call the piece 'Sad and Happy Music'.

Start with the sad section. You might like to make a wash of sound, scraping nails around the skins of drums and/or tambourines (laid flat on the floor), playing shakers with an upside down stirring movement, gently scraping guiros and playing small cymbals with soft beaters (very gently on the edge). If you have a child who is able to exercise restraint, so as not to create a loud, insistent tone, which would jar with the otherwise soft, smooth tone(!), ask them to play the occasional soulful chime on a pair of finger chimes. (Make sure the chimes are not in contact with any part of the child's body or they won't ring.)

Encourage the children to listen to the overall sound as they play. After say twenty seconds of this, you clap your hands to a medium beat to cue the children to play their instruments more loudly and joyfully in time with your beat. (You might like to have a change of instrument from the cymbals and finger chimes to, for example, claves and woodblocks.)

Talk about the music afterwards. Was everyone looking at you ready to change to happy music at the right time? Did anyone feel happy themselves when the music changed? Did the first part of the music make you feel sad?

Fast as a ferret

Mrs Drabble said Jake was 'as fast as a ferret'. Talk about what a ferret is.

Can you find other similes – fast as a…

What about the following:
Slow as a…
Heavy as a…
Light as a…
Funny as a…
Wise as a…
Tall as a…
Tiny as a…

Make a class book

Can you make a simple class picture bo[ok] out of the story *A Week in the Life of Tommy Mac*? Or take any character out of the story, e.g. the ferret, the spider, and create a whole new story for that creature or person.

A picture of me!

The children are going to try self-portraits with the help of mirrors. They should look in the mirror and feel the shape of their heads, then draw their eyes and feel that their nose starts between their eyes. They should feel their ears at the side of their heads and notice that their eyes are in line with the tops of their ears. Continue in this way, adding more detail according to ability.

Meanings and messages

Talk about this story. Tommy and Jake have lots of feelings in it. When did Tommy and Jake have warm fuzzy feelings and when did they have cold prickly feelings? Why?

Talk about why Tommy didn't like Jake, and then how the DVD that he saw helped him to realise something about Jake. What was it? Talk about misunderstandings in friendships, body language, facial expression.

How do all these things give messages? It's important to try to give the right message.

Talk about other stories that you have read together. Does every story have a message? Can you find the messages in simple stories such as *The Very Hungry Caterpillar*?

Talk about authors who make up the stories, and illustrators who help your imagination with their pictures.

Show how you feel

Try saying the little poem below, putting on the appropriate expression each time. Look at each other when you make the different expressions to see how other people show the emotions with their faces.

I'm feeling grumpy, I'm feeling grumpy. This is my grumpy face. (*Expression*)

I'm feeling happy, I'm feeling happy. This is my happy face. (*Expression*)

I'm feeling angry...

I'm feeling miserable...

I'm feeling scared...

I'm feeling puzzled...

Can the children think of any other words for the given words, e.g. cross, sad, frightened, muddled? Did the children notice how their voices change as well as their facial expressions when they are showing the various emotions?

Practise saying the words below in various voices appropriate to the various emotions — happy, sad, scared etc.

This is how I feel,
This is how I feel,
Can you guess how I feel?

Now ask one child to go out of sight or alternatively ask the other children to hide their eyes. The chosen child thinks of a feeling and whispers it to you. They then say the above words in the appropriate voice for their chosen emotion. Can the others guess from the tone of voice which emotion it is?

CD Track Listing

1. Song: We're Sailing Down The River (vocal)
2. Song: We're Sailing Down The River (backing track)
3. 'The Tortoise' from *Carnival Of The Animals* by Saint Saëns
4. 'The Mules' from *Carnival Of The Animals* by Saint Saëns
5. Song: There's A Dragon In The Sky (vocal)
6. Song: There's A Dragon In The Sky (backing track)
7. Let's Move!
8. Song: Sounds Outside (vocal)
9. Song: Sounds Outside (backing track)
10. How many sounds?
11. Song: The Extra Special Giant (vocal)
12. Song: The Extra Special Giant (backing track)
13. Song: Football Is The Game For Us! (vocal)
14. Song: Football Is The Game For Us! (backing track)
15. 'Trumpet and Drum' from *Children's Games* by Bizet
16. The Baking Song – 'We're going to make a cake'
17. Song: It's Just A Trick! (vocal)
18. Song: It's Just A Trick! (backing)
19. Song: Grumpy Stomps And Happy Jumps (vocal)
20. Song: Grumpy Stomps And Happy Jumps (backing)

12345678